MW01193419

# WHY SHOULD I CARE ABOUT BEETHOVEN?

## A BIOGRAPHY OF LUDWIG VAN BEETHOVEN JUST FOR KIDS!

SAM ROGERS

KidLit-O Books

ANAHEIM, CALIFORNIA

# Contents

# About KidLit-O

KidLit-O is an imprint of BookCaps™ that is just for kids! Each month BookCaps will be releasing several books in this exciting imprint. Visit our website or like us on Facebook to see more!

To add your name to our mailing list, visit this link: http://www.kidlito.com/mailing-list.html

# [1]

# INTRODUCTION

If you have ever studied classical music before, you will surely have heard of this name: Ludwig van Beethoven. Even today, almost two hundred years after his death, he stands as one of the most famous musical composers of all time—and for good reason! Beethoven was an extraordinary composer in the era of a classical music, creating music that is still listened to and played, even today. If you choose to study music, you might even end of playing something that he wrote!

A great composer is not always someone who makes great music; if that were the case, there would be more famous musicians than we can count. Often, a musician whose name is remembered for hundreds of years made changes in the world of music; they tried new things and wrote songs unlike those anyone had heard before. This is exactly what Beethoven did. However, there is something that is rather remarkable about Ludwig van Beethoven. He had a disability that most people thought would hinder his ability to play the piano and write music. He was deaf. So, with this disability, how did he become one of the greatest composers the world has ever known? You'll have to read on to find out.

# [2]

# EARLY CHILDHOOD

After the middle of the 1700s, there lived a young man named Johann van Beethoven. His father's name was Ludwig van Beethoven, although he liked to be called Louis, and Louis was a famous musician. Their family was Dutch, their name was well known, they were paid well, and they were talented. Grandfather Louis worked in the castle in the city of Cologne, Germany. His official title was "Kapellmeister," which means that he was in charge of the music for the court's church and such.

Johann looked up to grandfather Louis, and also studied music extensively. During this time period, sons would usually inherit their fathers' jobs. For example, a blacksmith's son would become a blacksmith, a chef's son would become a chef, and a musician's son would become a musician. Johann had his life set before him.

After also beginning work in the castle at Cologne, Johann went head-over-heels for a young woman. Her name was Maria Magdalena Keverich. However, Grandfather Louis was not too thrilled about this idea. Maria's late father had been an unimportant man, a chef. Louis thought that two people from different social classes should not marry that musicians were far better than chefs. Nevertheless, Johann and Maria went through with their marriage.

And thank goodness they did! After getting married, Johann and Maria seven children. When wondering what to name one of them, they thought they would him after his grandfather. Ludwig—it would be the perfect name: Ludwig van Beethoven.

Little Ludwig was born in the city of Bonn on the 16th of December 1770. He had six other siblings, but unfortunately, during this time, not many children made it out of childhood. Disease and sickness raged everywhere, due to unsanitary conditions. It was rather a miracle that Ludwig van Beethoven survived at all.

Because Louis was the Kapellmeister to the castle of Cologne, he was paid quite well; after all, he was musically talented! The same, however, could not be said for Johann. Johann taught music, yes, but he was never on the same level as his father. The whole family relied upon Louis for money. Without Louis's help, it would have been terribly hard for the Beethoven family to get by.

It should be noted that Beethoven was not born deaf; that came later on. For now, though, his hearing was perfectly fine. Like his grandfather Louis, Beethoven loved music. This was something that Johann and Louis were extremely proud of; as any parent does, they hoped he would be bright and successful one day. Little did thy know quite how successful he would actually be.

Ludwig van Beethoven was a quiet child. Of course, he occasionally liked to play, but he also just liked to sit and keep to his thoughts. He loved looking at mountains and rivers and the pretty colors of the sky. Germany has a fantastic array of scenery, so it was perfect for him. He could sit for hours and just watch the countryside, absolutely fascinated by it all.

When he was eight years old, he began his schoolwork. By this point, he was already playing music on the piano, something that was astounding. By today's standards, it would have been quite a sight to see! Immediately, his family could see that he had some real, true talent in him, and they needed to do everything they could to make sure Beethoven got the best education. It is often said that Johann wanted his son to become the next Wolfgang Amadeus Mozart—another famous musician. After hearing Beethoven's first concert at the age of eight, Johann knew right away that Beethoven needed more music teachers.

Beethoven's next teacher was a man called Van Den Eden. He played the organ at the castle court, and he was one of Louis's close friends. It soon became clear, however, that Beethoven knew far more than Van Den Eden and that the classes were pointless. Van Den Eden was let go, and Johann set out to find a new teacher.

He found a man who went by the name of Tobias Pfeiffer. Tobias was one of Johann's good friends, and they would often see each other in the bars at night. Tobias and a man named Christian G. Neefe both taught Beethoven at the same time, but they were not exactly the best teachers. Sometimes, Beethoven would be calmly sleeping at night when his door would suddenly burst open, and one of his teachers would storm in. They would claim that it was time to practice.

Beethoven got out of bed, but he was not necessarily upset. He enjoyed practicing, no matter what time of night it was. However, Johann was not a fan of Tobias's behavior. When Tobias finally left the city of Bonn, it almost came as a relief to the Beethoven family that the strange man was finally gone. No more midnight piano lessons! The teachers had still been essential to Beethoven's education, however. Without them, Bach might not have published his first piece of music at the age of twelve. It is called "Nine Variations on a March by Dressler." The piece was modeled after a march that was written by a composer named Earnst Cristoph Dressler. You could say that the published work was an arrangement, rather than a composition.

You see, when musicians write, they can do one of two things. They can either arrange or compose.

When a musician arranges, they take someone else's work and change it (with permission, of course). For example, if a man writes a song for only string instruments (like the violin and cello), but someone else wants to play it with his concert band (with instruments like trombones and tubas and clarinets and saxophones), then he will have to arrange the song, and write music for all of the other instruments. Arranging is usually easier than composing because you already have the building blocks for your piece.

Composing is starting from scratch. You have to write everything yourself. As you can probably imagine, this is a fantastic deal harder. It takes years of practice and months of work to make a single song. Most musicians start arranging as practice and then begin composing on their own once they're ready. It's like using training wheels first, to teach you the basics, and then you kick off on your own once you've had enough training.

When Beethoven was ten years old, he was playing the piano, the viola, and the violin. Three instruments and school—it was crazy! Not many kids, even in this time period, has this much level of work. And since Beethoven's family was a family of musicians, his skill was held to a high standard. Many scholars argue that it was unfair how much work Beethoven had to do—but nevertheless, he stuck through most of it.

When he was eleven years old, in the year 1781, he decided he did not want to go to regular school anymore. He already knew that he was going to be a musician—so why not direct his attention towards that? In addition to the piano, violin, and viola, he picked up the organ. Beethoven studied at a monastery in town, with a man named Brother Willibald Koch. The man was a friar who studied the life of St. Francis. Willibald was skilled at the organ, and he was more than happy to teach Beethoven everything he knew.

With that, Willibald Koch invited Beethoven to become his assistant. Beethoven was thrilled! After spending some time under Willibald's wing, he went on to become assistant of a man named Zenser. Zenser was the official organist at the town chapel. Beethoven was not yet fifteen years old, and he was already one of the most important musicians in town.

Something incredible happened when Beethoven was fourteen years old. His old teacher, Christian G. Neefe found out that the castle at Cologne was looking for a new organist. The Elector at the castle, also the prince, was named Maximillian Franz. The castle was a totally different world to the one that Beethoven had known. He was now seeing important people on a daily basis and playing the organ for them. His father was not only extremely proud, but a little jealous too. His son was doing everything that he had wanted to do as a musician.

In fact, Johann was not doing so well at home. He was drinking more alcohol and was not attentive to his children. For this reason, not only was Grandfather Louis supporting the family, but now Beethoven was, as well. Some of his paychecks went towards the family and helping them get by. In today's age, this might seem like a lot to expect out of a fifteen year-old boy, but it was almost common during Beethoven's time.

# [3]

# KEEPING UP WITH MOZART AND OTHER TEACHERS

Two years later, when he was seventeen years old, Ludwig van Beethoven traveled to the city of Vienna, the capital of the country of Austria. He knew almost immediately that he wanted to stay here. The trip took several weeks to plan since he did not know exactly when he might return to his home in Bonn. There was one key reason why Beethoven chose Vienna as a destination: it was, supposedly, where the famed musician Wolfgang Amadeus Mozart was staying. In his wildest dreams, Beethoven imagined himself taking lessons with the celebrity.

By this point in his life, people had started talking about Beethoven. When he was eleven, he traveled to Holland. A few years after that, he became the official organist to the Prince of Cologne; his name was talked about in circles of musicians everywhere. No doubt that Mozart would have heard his name, and even wanted to hear the young organist play a tune himself. When Prince Maximillian Franz heard that Beethoven wanted to travel to Vienna to see Mozart, he was thrilled. Immediately he wrote a letter for Beethoven to take with him, a letter that said how excellent Beethoven was. It was meant to be delivered to Mozart.

The trip from Bonn to Vienna, about 550 miles, took Beethoven one month to travel. Some estimates say that, by car, the trip would take about nine hours across the European countryside. Upon his arrival in Vienna, he ordered a room at a hotel and immediately traveled to Mozart's house and was taken inside. He was told Mozart would be with him shortly.

Mozart finally met up, but it was done reluctantly. The famous composer, although not even thirty-five was ill. When his death could be upon him any day now, did he really have time to listen to some child, however famous, play his organ? He told Beethoven to sit down at the piano and play a song.

Beethoven panicked. The Mozart wanted him to play a song! He knew that he needed to play a song that would impress Mozart, so he started to play one of Mozart's piano concertos. But Mozart immediately stopped him, and said that he did not want to hear one of his own pieces. He wanted to hear Beethoven play something that he had wrote himself. Otherwise, how could Mozart judge the boy's talent properly?

When Beethoven was finished playing, Mozart stood up. While twenty minutes ago, he had been groaning at the idea of a boy coming into his house to play the piano, he was now stunned. Beethoven truly was something to talk about! He walked in to the next room and got his wife. He raved to his wife about how great of a player Beethoven was, and he predicted that this boy would one day become one of the most talked-about composers in the history of the world.

How right he was.

After seeing Beethoven's playing, Mozart wanted to make the boy his student. He saw some real talent here! Beethoven obviously agreed. It was like all of his dreams were coming true. Maybe he would actually be the next Mozart!

Happy, Beethoven went back to his hotel. When he got there, however, he found an urgent message from his father. Beethoven needed to return to Bonn as quickly as he could. His mother Maria was dying of illness, and the doctors did not think that she would last too much longer.

The choice was easy. Beethoven needed to leave Vienna. He needed to see his mother, just in case this illness was as serious as the doctors predicted it was. When he finally arrived once again in Bonn, he learned that his mother had died during his journey.

It devastated Beethoven since she was one of his most supportive influences, usually better than his father Johann. Beethoven decided that his lessons with Mozart would have to wait a few years; right now, he actually needed to be with his family, especially with heartbroken siblings. However, in 1791, Beethoven was struck again.

Wolfgang Amadeus Mozart's illness finally got to him, and he died on December 5th, 1791. Beethoven had not taken a single lesson with him. As you can probably imagine, his dreams were crushed by yet another death. Beethoven would never get to be his apprentice. Despite this, however, he returned to Vienna the next year to find the city in mourning for the lost great composer.

If he did not find a true mentor in Mozart, he did find one in Franz Joseph Haydn, another famous composer. Haydn also lived in Vienna, and he was happy to take Beethoven in. After all, Mozart and Haydn had known each other, and Haydn had heard about the bright child prodigy.

Haydn arranged for Beethoven to stay in the home of Prince Lichnowsky of Vienna, a hugely prestigious place. Beethoven and the prince became fast friends, which was a huge advantage to Beethoven. As they say, making connections is the key to success. In a world where it is tough to become a famous musician, having friends in high places is not a bad thing.

Unfortunately, however, Haydn did not stay in Vienna for too long. Three years after Beethoven returned to Vienna, Haydn traveled to London for other studies. In his place stood a man named Johann Georg Albrechtsberger, who was the organist at the castle in Vienna. To play with such an important musician was an honor; sure, he was no Mozart, but on a daily basis Albrechtsberger interacted with the higher-up officials in Austria's government. And now Beethoven was there! If only his mother could see him, she would have been extremely proud. He had surely worked his way up from the bottom on his talent. Those days and nights of practicing the piano certainly paid off!

At the same time that Beethoven learned to play instruments and performed in the court of Vienna and for Prince Lichnowsky, he also needed to practice his vocal skills. Even today, it is said that, "If you can sing it, you can play it." Many concert bands and marching bands sing for a warm-up because it helps the players adjust to the sound and play better. Try it, it works!

There was one man in Vienna truly suited to teach Beethoven everything he needed to know about singing, and his name was Antonio Salieri. But Antonio had an interesting past; he was one of Wolfgang Amadeus Mozart's rivals. The two of them often competed for performances and fame. In fact, there was such heated competition between the two of them that some people believed Salieri poisoned Mozart.

Just before his death, Mozart wondered if he had been poisoned (despite having been sick for several years). Even in later years, when Salieri was dying, he claimed to have poisoned Mozart—but the majority of people did not believe him since he was delusional. All of that aside, however, it is possible that Beethoven had some reservations about training with Salieri. The fear of poison was ripe in his mind.

So Beethoven had two great musicians teaching him at the same. Under Albrechtsberger, he studied at the court of Vienna and played for princes, meanwhile learning how to sing under Antonio Salieri. The skills that Beethoven gained during these years were essential to his later works. It was the practice that helped hone his skills.

# [4]

# FROM THE CLASSICAL ERA TO THE ROMANTIC ERA

When historians look back at the times in which dinosaurs roamed the earth, they give a name to certain eras or periods, such as the Jurassic Period, the Triassic Period, and each era is defined by different dinosaurs. In the same way, historians give names to musical eras, depending on what type of music existed during that time.

In the year 1400, an exciting happened, today known as the Renaissance Era. Renaissance means "enlightenment," and it was a period of new and innovative ideas in the world of music, art, theater, and science. People were beginning to look at the world with logic and reason, and technology boomed, especially with the invention of the printing press.

The world of music was revamped, and in the year 1600 the Baroque Era started. One of the most famous musicians of the Baroque Era was Johann Sebastian Bach, and his death in 1750 marked the end of the Baroque Era. Thus began the era of classical music, one of the most famous and influential music periods in history.

Beethoven was born into the Classical period, so he grew up with the typical music of the time. Classical music is often defined by a few different things.

Mood Contrasts – The music in the Classical Era bounced between happy and sad. This helped make the music more interesting because there was never a dull moment. The audience never knew what turn a piece of music would take. It was truly revolutionary, after centuries of music that had stayed the same. This allowed for classical pieces to feel more emotional. In a movie, directors will often put happy and sad scenes next to each other for more impact. The musicians of the Classical Era had the same idea.

Simple Melodies – Music in the Classical Era was known for having simple melodies. When you think of classical music, you might think of long, confusing, perhaps even boring songs.

These songs can stretch anywhere from two minutes to over an hour. But no matter complicated they might be, you can always find a simple melody, a line of music that might repeat over and over again, played by different instruments or with different notes. Listen to a piece of classical music and see if you find the melody!

Dynamic Contrast – In a piece of music, the word "dynamics" is used to describe the volume of the piece. Soft dynamics are low volumes, and loud dynamics are high volumes. Music in the Classical Era was known for changing between soft and loud quickly, which went along well with the contrast in the mood. When a line of music gets louder, that is called a crescendo; when a line of music gets softer, that is called a decrescendo. Sometimes, musicians might use crescendos and decrescendo to gradually change the volume; otherwise, they might just put a sign in the music to tell the players to either immediately grow and immediately shrink volume.

In music, the word piano, besides being an instrument, means "soft," marked with a p. The next level up is metzopiano, which means "medium soft," marked with a mp. After that comes metzoforte, or "medium loud," marked with a mf. Then comes "forte," which just means loud, marked by f. After that, you can have ff, which means "very loud," fff, which means "extremely loud," or ffff, which means as loud as possible.

At the time, one of the most popular instruments was the harpsichord, one of the precursors to the piano. A notable player of the harpsichord is the famous composer of the Baroque period, Johann Sebastian Bach. However, the harpsichord did not do too well with such drastic dynamic changes. This was part of the reason the piano became so popular; it was much easier to switch from soft to loud.

The fact that composers were trying to incorporate more emotion into their music was key. This inevitably led to the Romantic Era after the death of Beethoven years later. During the Romantic Era, composers were inspired by nature and passionate emotions to create the most intense and deep music as possible. Today, Ludwig van Beethoven is seen as a stepping-stone between the Classical Era and the Romantic Era. For the most part, classical and romantic music are the same, even romanticism is more heavily loaded with emotion and feeling.

Beethoven's music was often emotional. Try listening to some of his pieces, and think about how they make you feel. You might be surprised how much a piece of music can move you!

Beethoven also enjoyed using bigger orchestras. More people meant more sound, and that was something that Beethoven liked. Before this time period, most bands and orchestras had been small, limited to only a few people commanding each instrument. With the growth of music during this period, however, there were more people to play, and Beethoven took advantage of this. He liked stretching the ranges of certain instruments, making the violins and the cellos play low notes, when they were typically used for higher pitches.

# [5]

# GROWING DEAF

This is one of the great ironies of Ludwig van Beethoven's life. Music mainly requires you to listen, and that is one of its joys. Sometimes we take listening to music for granted and pass it off like it is nothing. But the more we stop and think about it, it is incredible how someone can blow air through an instrument, slide a bow on a string, and pound a stick on a drum, and create something that will enter our ears and transmit through our minds as something beautiful.

So, how exactly did Beethoven start becoming deaf? He had a condition called tinnitus, which is when one hears a noise in their ears, like a ringing or a humming. It is said that Beethoven described the noise as a "roaring,", so his case was most likely more severe than most. It hurt to listen to things, and he often tried to avoid talking to people. Beethoven stopped sleeping well, he started getting angry, and it even interfered with his music. How was he supposed to work with all that roaring in his ears? He was certainly distressed.

Tinnitus is most often seen in people who have exposure to loud sounds. A good example of this might be a construction worker, who has to deal with jackhammers and pounding and the other sounds that go along with putting up a building. If someone is in a rock band, and they listen to loud guitars and drums all day, that can be painful and harmful to their hearing.

It started with tinnitus and evolved into deafness, but no one is quite sure how. It is clear that he had severe problems with his hearing. Not only must the tinnitus have been horrible to deal with, but the slow realization that he was growing deaf must have been devastating for him to handle. It would be like working as a writer and finding out you can't write anymore, and being a chef and finding out you can't cook anymore. The emotional distress for Beethoven must have been high.

At the first sign of deafness, he sent a letter to his family in Bonn, telling them everything. Things only got worse from there, and he needed to carry around a notebook so that people could write what they wanted to tell him. Obviously, he was embarrassed. What would the people say if they knew the famous musician Beethoven was growing deaf? He wanted to keep it a secret for as long as possible. He told his family to "keep the matter of my deafness a profound secret to be confided to nobody, no matter whom."

The descent into deafness took almost two years, which could have made the situation even more maddening. Some historians argue that, in the end, he was completely and utterly deaf, unable to hear a thing. Others argue that he could hear slightly, and maybe some days were better than others. No matter what the case is, though, it must have been horrible to deal with. He considered ending his life a few times, but thank goodness he did not!

Even though he grew more deaf, his talent did not shrink. He still composed lovely music for all to hear, which astounded his audiences. His hearing may have been gone, but not his mind. He could still write and remember what the notes sounded like. At the same time that he was going deaf, however, Europe was being taken by storm, by one of the most heroic and feared dictators of all time: Emperor Napoleon the First of France.

# [6]

# A SONATA IN THE MOONLIGHT

Before we take a look at Beethoven and Napoleon, however, let's take a look at one of Beethoven's most popular songs, written during this time period. It is called Moonlight Sonata; perhaps you have heard of it! To this day, it is one of the most downloaded pieces of classical music on the internet. If you ever play the piano, chances are that you will one day cross paths with the mysterious Moonlight Sonata.

As its name is mysterious, so is its music. But it was not always called "Moonlight Sonata." It's official title is "Piano Sonata No. 14 in C# minor," just a fancy way of classifying all of the songs that Beethoven wrote. He often called the song Quasi una fantasia, which translates to

"Almost a Fantasy." No one actually calls it that anymore, since its more popular title has taken full swing.

Even at the time that it was written, his audiences were infatuated with it. Try listening to it online; its melodies are beautiful, almost haunting, and it is a great example of a composer trying to put feeling and emotion into his work. After Beethoven wrote it, he could not understand why people liked it so much. He told one of his students, "[The people] are always talking about [Moonlight Sonata] ... surely I've written better things." He could not understand why his audiences were so infatuated with it.

Moonlight Sonata was published in 1801, exactly around the time when Beethoven was panicking about his gradually fading hearing. You can probably bet the sad, slow melodies in the beginning were probably inspired by some of the feelings of dread he was experiencing at the time. As we know, he started spending less time with other people because conversation hurt his hearing. He would retreat into his house and sometimes refuse to come out. Writing Moonlight Sonata was one the songs that helped him practice his musical ability despite hearing loss.

However, if you listen to the whole sonata, you will find that the eerie and sad music at the beginning, the tone changes drastically after about six minutes. It becomes happy and bouncy, and there is a clear reason for this.

We know that it was typical for songs of the day to change quickly from sad to happy, and vice versa. This is true for Moonlight Sonata, but Beethoven did not make it that way just to fit the requirements for a piece of music in the classical era. The beginning is supposed to represent his dread and fear, and the happy part represents his triumph over that fear. Even in his Fifth Symphony, which you will learn about soon enough, the beginning starts off rough and frightening, but the ending is joyous and grand.

This is where music stops becoming just notes on a page and can tell us so much more about the composer's life. If the beginning represents his unhappiness and fear, then the ending represents not only his overcoming of the fear, but also the fact that he continued to pump out amazing songs. For this reason, and because the music itself is gorgeous, Moonlight Sonata is one of the most popular classical songs ever written.

As he continued to deal with the loss of his hearing, Beethoven had a heap of other problems on his plate. For one, he was living in a world in which Europe was slowly consumed with revolution and conquest at the hands of a dictator, one whose name would be revered by some and feared by all.

# [7]

# BEETHOVEN AND THE EMPEROR

In order to understand Beethoven and his music, we also have to understand the world that he lived in. It was a world of progress, of new advances in music. It was a world of technology, where the world was making huge strides in factories and machines. But it was also a world of revolution and war, and coming from the country of France was a man whose name would go down in history as both a hero and a villain. His name was Napoleon the First, Emperor of France.

In the year 1796, when Beethoven was twenty-six years old, Napoleon Bonaparte was appointed to head the French army in Italy. The French were trying to get back at the British, who had two big allies: Austria and Russia. But before he worried about his three enemies, the commander returned to France to handle several rebellions that were sprouting about. The people were trying to rise against the government, which they saw as evil. Napoleon took over the government and made himself Emperor.

Now, despite the fact that Beethoven lived in Austria, and Napoleon was enemies with that country, Beethoven had a soft spot for the commander. He supported Napoleon's efforts to help overthrow the ridiculous French government. He believed that the French needed a more efficient form of government and that Napoleon was the man to organize it.

But Beethoven did not support Napoleon crowning himself emperor. In his eyes, this meant that Napoleon was power-hungry. When he discovered this horrifying news, Beethoven cried out, "So he is no more than a common mortal! Now, too, he will tread under foot all the rights of man, indulge only his ambition; now he will think himself superior to all men, become a tyrant!"

Beethoven was especially disheartened by the news. He had been writing a symphony in the name of Napoleon since he was so inspired. Beethoven ripped up the title page of the symphony. Whatever its previous title was, Beethoven changed it to "Eroica." There was no way he would write a symphony to the Emperor of France.

In the year 1809, when Beethoven was thirty-nine years old, the forces of Emperor Napoleon the First invaded Vienna. The citizens fled from the power of the French army, and Beethoven hid in his brother's basement; his brother also lived in Vienna. Cannons fired everywhere, guns shooting bullets left and right. The loud noises were especially tough on Beethoven's sensitive ears. Even in deafness, the tinnitus hurt him when loud sounds were around.

After the invasion of Vienna, Beethoven wrote a concerto that is now called "Emperor." He did not give it that name, but it came many years later. Beethoven would have hated the name "Emperor" for one of his concertos, especially because he equated that with Emperor Napoleon.

Nevertheless what it is called, the "Emperor" Concerto was Beethoven's final completed, and greatest concerto. It is also known as Beethoven's Fifth Concerto, and it follows many of the styles of classical music. There are many changes from soft volumes to loud volumes, very quickly. This catches the interest of the audience. Go on the internet and take a listen to Beethoven's Emperor Concerto. It's an excellent piece of musical literature!

It is a common myth that Beethoven disliked Napoleon forever; as time wore on, he slowly began to like the emperor again. When Napoleon finally died, Beethoven said it was a "catastrophe." No matter how Beethoven truly felt about the Emperor of France throughout his life, the historical backdrop is crucial, and the music that came out of this time period is invigorating. It is difficult to imagine the state that Beethoven was in, with the loss of his eyesight on hand and the rise of Emperor Napoleon on the other.

It is said that Beethoven, in the year 1811, two years after the invasion of Vienna, attempted to perform the Emperor Concerto in public. Seeing as most of Beethoven's hearing was gone, however, this must have been an incredibly daunting task—and indeed, it was a failed one. It went horribly, and some people say that, after this, Beethoven never played for an audience again.

During this turbulent time period, Beethoven wrote a song that is still popular with piano players. You have probably heard it before, but might not be able to put a name to it. It is called Für Elise, which just means "For Elise" in English. Like many of Beethoven's pieces, Für Elise is known across the world, even almost two centuries after Beethoven's death.

Beethoven wrote the song in the year 1810, around the time that he was working on the Emperor Concerto. Clearly, many things were running through Beethoven's mind at the time! It is crucial to note that Beethoven did not name the song Für Elise, however. The mysterious name came later, after he died.

The song was found among Beethoven's collections, with the words Für Elise on them. Apparently, Beethoven had been thinking about someone named Elise and wanted to dedicate the piece to her. The song is hauntingly beautiful; it is definitely worth a listen! Many people wonder whether Elise was someone that Beethoven was in love with, but historians have something else to say.

Historians claim that, at the time the song was written, Beethoven was in love with a woman named Therese Malfatti. They know this from some of his journal entries and letters. Because of this, some people believe that the handwriting on the original copies of the song were misread and that Beethoven actually wrote Für Therese, and not Für Elise. However, there is no solid proof, and this is only a theory. It keeps the mystery going!

In 2009, almost two hundred years after the song was written, a man named Klaus Martin Kopitz, a Beethoven specialist, said that, at the time, Beethoven was not in love with a woman named Therese Malfatti, but instead he was still thinking about a woman that he had met a few years ago: a woman named Elisabeth Röckel. If this is the case, then it is likely that Elise was just a nickname for Elisabeth.

It is sad that this piece never became particularly popular during Beethoven's lifetime since he never published it. If it is still so popular today, one can only imagine how people might have responded in Beethoven's time. The people would have gone wild! No matter who Für Elise was actually written for, it still stands as one of the most beautiful and popular musical compositions in history. Beethoven was truly a genius!

# [8]

# THE FIFTH

The song commonly known as Beethoven's Fifth is most definitely one of his most popular songs. Chances are you may have heard it played in cartoons before, at a concert, or in the theme song to the popular show Judge Judy. There is no doubt that the song continues to exist in our world today—but why? Why is it so noteworthy? What did it mean to Beethoven, and what does it mean to us now? Why did he write it, and when?

Beethoven started getting ideas for the song around the time he began losing his hearing. He often said that it was "Fate" that made him lose his hearing, and that it was bursting through his door to torment him. You can definitely compare this idea with the loud and shocking beginning of Beethoven's Fifth (a few words on a page can only describe it as da-da-

da DUMMMM). Today, the beginning of the song in a cartoon usually signals a giant "uh-oh" moment—well, it did for Beethoven too.

It took the composer four years to write the Fifth. He started in 1804 and finished somewhere 1808, before the invasion of Vienna by the newly self-crowned Emperor Napoleon. People were not thrilled with it at first; they were much too-consumed with some of his other amazing works to bother with the Fifth. Only over a longer space of time did people realize that Beethoven's Fifth was incredible.

The first few notes of the song are no doubt the most famous and well known part. Today, it might be because it introduces a feeling of foreboding and horror. But in Beethoven's time, people were awed of it because it started with three short notes (da-da-da) followed by a heavy long note (DUMMMM). This shocked them! It was so different from any of the music of the day, so jarring and unexpected that the audience could not help but stay and listen. The notes are from the first movement of the piece; in fact, there are four movements. The first one is called Allegro con brio, which means "fast, with spirit."

Today, along with putting the song into various cartoons across television and on the internet, you can find a funk / jazz arrangement of Beethoven's Fifth, performed by Walter Murphy and the Big Apple Band, and even a remix between Beethoven's Fifth and Kanye West's "Gold Digger." The song has endured almost two centuries of performances, and it will most certainly continue this trend in the future.

# [9]

# BEETHOVEN'S LATER YEARS

In the years after Napoleon's rise and fall as Emperor of France, Beethoven was in a flurry of musical writing. Being dead did not stop him in the slightest from recovering quickly and going on with his music. Sure, it was much harder. But he got through it.

He even fell in love many times. Some people say that Ludwig van Beethoven was a hopeless romantic, always in love but never seeming to find the right girl. Love was always a bit of a struggle for him. Scholars have maintained some of the love notes that Beethoven wrote to a girl named Eleonore van Breuning, a daughter of a family friend. The van Breuning family helped out a lot when Beethoven's mother died, and Beethoven fell in love with their daughter. It was not to last, however.

In his path, he also found the lovely Magdalena Willman, a singer at the time. Beethoven harbored passionate feelings for Magdalena, and he always wondered how he might tell her. He knew her before he went deaf. When he ultimately told her his true feelings, she flat out denied him. She told Beethoven that he was ugly and crazy, not something that Beethoven exactly wanted to hear. It was a depressing piece of news for the hopeless romantic.

After Beethoven's death, historians found a love letter that he had wrote, addressed to someone only known as "The Immortal Beloved." Since no specific name was mentioned, we can only guess who Beethoven was writing to. Many women claimed to be the one, but no one can be one hundred percent sure. In fact, the mystery of Beethoven's secret love is so intense that a movie was made in 1994 about it. It is an R-rated movie called Immortal Beloved, starring Gary Oldman, who children might recognize as Sirius Black from the Harry Potter films.

Towards the end of 1815, one of Beethoven's brothers passed away, leaving behind his wife Johanna and his son Karl. His brother's dying wish was that Beethoven would take care of Karl, but Johanna did not think that was a great idea. But Beethoven was not going up on his brother's dying wish; he took his words seriously. He would do everything in his power to take care of Karl.

Johanna was furious, and soon she and Beethoven were in court. Johanna wanted to take care of Karl because she knew that was the rightful mother, but Beethoven said it went against his brother's final command, and that Johanna was not the best-suited mother. It took five years for the case to end, and Beethoven was granted custody of the child. Torn away from her child, Johanna continued to seek custody from the courts, to no avail, however.

Finding himself without a wife and a child to take care of, Beethoven was determined to give Karl a good life. Like himself, Karl liked to play music, though he was not good; but beyond that, Beethoven and Karl found it very difficult to connect to each other.

Karl was fourteen years old when he left his mother and entered the home of his Uncle Ludwig. If you do not have parents who have gone through a divorce, or experienced the death of a parent, it is difficult to imagine the pain. Karl suddenly lost two of his parents, one still living, and was now in the hands of an uncle that he had rarely seen. What was he to do? Things were made worse when Beethoven told him he was not allowed, under any circumstances, to visit his mother. Beethoven clearly was not the biggest fan of Johanna, and he didn't want Karl near her.

Karl, though, did not listen to his uncle. On more than one occasion, Beethoven would suddenly find Karl gone, and knew that the boy had escaped to visit his mother. Since this was not allowed by the law, however, Beethoven contacted the police, and they went to retrieve him. Neither Karl nor Johanna was too happy about this, but it was the way things were.

Beethoven felt like a father to Karl, despite their rough relationship. As mentioned before, he took his role as Karl's protector seriously. He never wanted to let his brother down while he was living, and he would certainly not let his brother down after his death.

To occupy Karl's time, Beethoven sent him to a number of schools. Since Beethoven had never had a child himself, this was his opportunity to be a father; to make sure that Karl was sent to the right schools, got the best education, and was instructed by only the best teachers. Beethoven himself was teaching a number of students in Vienna, one of them named Carl Czerny.

Beethoven told Karl that Czerny would be his new musical instructor, but there was only small problem. After a few lessons, Czerny came to the conclusion that Karl had no musical talent whatsoever, and it was impossible that he would ever learn an instrument. Beethoven thought this was preposterous. The Beethovens were known for their music! He would hear none of it. He ordered Czerny to keep on with the lessons, despite the fact that Karl hated them.

So, it was quite clear that Karl was not going to become the great musician that Beethoven expected him to be. Quite the opposite, really. Karl attended the University of Vienna to study philology. Philology is the study of language in documents, especially historical documents. Philologists are often interested in both history, and how languages work. In addition to this, Karl wanted to go into the military. When he told Beethoven this, Beethoven was furious. Especially after the rise of Emperor Napoleon, seeing his nephew in the military was the last thing he wanted to see.

# [10]

# ODE TO JOY!

Even more popular than Beethoven's Fifth Symphony is most likely his ninth. Beethoven's Ninth Symphony is often called "Ode to Joy," and for a great reason! The song is happy and joyous. The word "ode" means a "tribute" or a "song to." The title indicates that it was written purely for happiness.

Beethoven composed his Ninth Symphony sometime between the years 1822 and 1824; what is unique is that so a happy a piece could have been written when Beethoven was so distraught over his relationship with his nephew. The song was dedicated to the King of Prussia at the time, a man named Friedrich Wilhelm III.

The song was instantly popular. People loved to listen to it! Today, we may take CDs and computers for advantage. We have iPods and phones and MP3 players that let us listen to music whenever we want; people in Beethoven's time were not so lucky. They really only heard music unless they attended a concert or they played it themselves, or if someone in the family practiced in the house. For this reason, people went wild over the Ninth Symphony. It was unlike anything they had ever heard before! The song is still happy, and it too appears in movies and television shows as a signal of triumph and success.

At the time, and this is particularly typical of the Romantic Era, musicians tried to write music that would fit poetry and paintings. The Ode to Joy was written to fit a poem written by a man named Friedrich Schiller, a poem called "Ode to Joy." The lines that Beethoven had in mind are: "Man is to all men a brother, Which embraces all beings! A kiss to all the world." This just means that we are all brothers, and we must all be kind to each other. This was one of the key ideals that Emperor Napoleon of France originally fought for. The main slogan for the French Revolution was Liberté, Egalité, Fraternité, which means Liberty, Equality, and Brotherhood. This idea of "brotherhood" was something that Beethoven understood and respected, especially considering how well he honored his dying brother's wishes by taking care of Karl.

Despite the fact that the symphony had been officially composed starting in 1822, the ideas for it had been toiling around in Beethoven's head since 1809, when Napoleon invaded Vienna.

Throughout history, Ode to Joy has been played at many historical events. This goes to show that, even decades after its writing, Beethoven's Ninth remains one of the most famous classical compositions of all time.

It has been played at Olympic ceremonies, to highlight the joy of the event and push for international companionship. One of the most beautiful things about music is that it can bring together people from all countries and who speak all languages. It does not matter that Ode to Joy was written by a German composer; people across Asia, Australia, the Americas, Africa, and Europe enjoy it too!

After the Second World War in 1945, a large divided east and west Germany. There were two separate governments; the east was supported by Russia (which was called the Soviet Union back then), and the west was supported by the United States. The United States and the Soviet Union were in a fierce competition to see who could gather more nuclear weapons or travel to space first. For five decades, there were many instances where World War III could have broken out at any moment, initiated by this feud between the U.S. and the Soviet Union. This period of time was known as the Cold War; people called it "cold," because no fighting actually took place, but people were waiting for the war to "thaw" and "warm up" and become a heated battle.

When the wall that divided east and west Germany, known as the Berlin Wall, finally was destroyed in 1989, a large celebration was held. Chunks of the fallen wall were boxed and are sold as historical artifacts. Beethoven's Ninth was played at the event, because of its happy tone and message of unity.

Ode to Joy is also the official anthem of the European Union, the organization that unites most European countries, including: Austria, Belgium, Bulgaria, Croatia, Cyrprus, the Czech Republic, Denmark, Estonia, Finland, France, Germany, Greece, Hungary, Iceland, Italy, Latvia, Lithuania, Luxembourg, Malta, the Netherlands, Poland, Portugal, Romania, Slovakia, Slovenia, Spain, Sweden, and the United Kingdom (which includes England, Ireland, Scotland, and Wales). These are a lot of countries, and you could say that Ode to Joy is their theme song. What do you think Beethoven would say if he knew this? He would probably be humbled and amazed.

Many Americans probably heard the playing of "Ode to Joy" after the attack on New York City's World Trade Center on September 11th, 2001. Despite the fact that over two thousand lives were lost, Americans joined together and united, with the support of many countries across the globe. In the wake of the attack, the song Ode to Joy was used to demonstrate that America would heal in triumph, even in the face of horror and fear. Once again, Beethoven's Ninth proved that the song has an eternal and hopeful message: we are all brothers and friends, and we can survive any hardship. This is one of the reasons that Ode to Joy will live on forever.

It is great to study the effect that Ode to Joy had on a history, and even the effect that history had on Ode to Joy. It is also important to note the impact that the song had on future musicians. Countless musical celebrities of the time listen to Beethoven's Ninth and were astounded! Most notable among them were Schubert and Brahms, who would go on to become famous composers.

Despite all of these great things, however, not everyone exactly likes the Ode to Joy, or its happy messages. Some people think that the world is too sad for the song to provide us with any true happiness, and it only provides false hope. But throughout history, time and time again, Beethoven's Ninth Symphony has helped people heal with grief, as it most certainly helped Beethoven at the time.

Over time, singers were added to the piece. Typical with how Beethoven liked to compose, the piece is meant for more than a small band of a dozen musicians. Perhaps the largest recorded performance of Ode to Joy in 10,000 singers and players in a stadium. On the internet, you can also find a fascinating video where a lone cello plays "Ode to Joy" in a park, and is suddenly joined by instruments of all varieties. It was a planned event, meant purely as an entertainment stunt.

No matter what you might think of Ode to Joy, whether you think it's boring, whether you think it is naïve, or whether you think it is one of the greatest musical compositions of all time, it is hard to debate the importance of the song throughout history. In the tough times for Beethoven ahead, it was crucial that he cling

onto the idea of victory and triumph to help
him through the pain.

# [11]

# THE DEATH AND LEGACY OF LUDWIG VAN BEETHOVEN

By the time 1826 rolled around, Karl was a distraught mess. His fifty-six year old Uncle Ludwig was way too controlling. He wanted to see his mother, and he wanted to live his life without his uncle being upset at him. Karl was so upset that he wanted to end his life. His landlord, the person who rented out his home to him, told Beethoven about this.

Beethoven panicked, as any father or uncle would do. Little did he know, but Karl was running away with two guns and a load of gunpowder. Beethoven tried to track his nephew, with extreme difficulty. Meanwhile, Karl had climbed to the top of a set of ruins in the German city of Baden. They were called the Rauhenstein Ruins, and Beethoven and Karl would often walk through here. He thought this would be the perfect place to end his life.

Hands shaking, Karl tried to shoot himself—but missed. The second time, the bullet found his target. Karl was shot, but he did not die. Beethoven found the poor boy, distraught and practically unconscious on top of the Rauhenstein Ruins. He took Karl back to town, while the boy begged to be taken to his mother's house.

Karl did not stay with his mother for long, but you can imagine how Johanna reacted to seeing her son like this. He was taken to the hospital, and Johanna accused Beethoven of being a horrible guardian. Beethoven took this all hard, and many historians believe that he never recovered from the horror and pain of Karl's attempted suicide.

Once Karl was out of the hospital, he told his uncle that he was still going into the military, something that Beethoven did not want to believe. Little did he know that, the moment Karl left, this would be the final time he would see his nephew. It was not an emotional departure, as you might think, with crying and opposite. Exactly the opposite. Karl knew that Beethoven had been feeling sick lately, especially after more than twenty years with tinnitus.

When Karl left for the German military, Beethoven was staying with his brother Johann. Unfortunately, Johann and Beethoven had never actually gotten along well. The death of their brother and the attempted suicide of the rebellious Karl had created a rift between them. Johann demanded that if his brother Ludwig van Beethoven was going to stay with him for a while, then he was going to pay rent.

Beethoven was furious! This was his brother! In times of distress, the two brothers should have overlooked their differences and united. Instead, Beethoven decided to leave his brother's house and return to Vienna. But it was the beginning of December, the weather was freezing, and he had no way to get back except to ride on the back of a milkman's cart.

Upon his return to Vienna, Beethoven felt dangerously sick, most likely due to his freezing milkcart ride. He knew that he needed to write his will immediately. A will is someone's last wishes. Beethoven needed to dictate who would get his house, who would get his belongings, and who would receive all of his money after he died. After his argument and falling out with his brother Johann, he was not too keen to let anything go to him.

Instead, he decided all of his stuff would go to someone even more unlikely: his nephew Karl, the one man that he thought of as a son. Beethoven did not have a ton of money; he was not wealthy. The London Philharmonic Society, who knew how talented he was and that he had fallen on rough times, had donated some money to him.

A little less than four months after his return to Vienna, Ludwig van Beethoven was lying on his deathbed. He knew that his time was near, and he was glad that he already had his will sorted out, although he would never see his nephew Karl again. His friend Anton Schindler came to his house to take care of him, along with the Breuning family, who had also been there for Beethoven's mother's death.

On the 26th of March in 1827, a terrible storm struck Vienna. The sky was alight with daunting clouds and crackling lightning. Thunder roared and rain checkered against the windowpane. It was on this night that Beethoven died, amidst the horrible storm. Once he died, the storm calmed and turned into a light snowstorm.

On the 28th of March, two days later, Beethoven was buried in Vienna, in a place called the Währing Cemetery. It was one of the grandest funerals that Vienna had ever seen. People from all across Germany flocked as quickly as they could to see the great composer buried. It is said that somewhere between ten thousand and thirty thousand people attended the funeral; most people put the number in the middle, at twenty thousand. Schools were even shut down for the day, so that everyone could pay their respects to the fallen musician.

So now that we've thoroughly explored the life and times of the famous composer Ludwig van Beethoven, we need to understand why he lives through history. Even though he died almost two hundred years ago, his music still lives on, and he still influences the musicians of today.

Beethoven is seen as one of the composers that led us from the Classical Era and into the Romantic Era, mainly because of how much emotion he put into his music. And he had plenty of reason to! Beethoven led a sad life. None of his relationships worked out, he never ended up as Mozart's student, he never had a wife or child, went deaf at twenty years old, his nephew hated him and tried to commit suicide, and he got into an argument with brother and caught a terrible cold that ended in death.

There was plenty for Beethoven to feel sad and angry about it, and a lot of this energized his music.

And despite all the trials and all the hardships that he endured, we can always find a happy message in his music. Sure, we may feel sad sometimes, but that does mean that our happiness cannot overcome that. This is a common theme in his music; sad melodies followed by bright happy ones. That is his message to us, one that he wants everyone to follow. Coming from a man who experienced so much during his life, it is a important message.

We have a lot to learn from Beethoven. Even though he was deaf, he still wrote some of the finest masterpieces the musical world has ever seen. In the face of daunting fear and pain, he stuck through it all, kept a smile on his face, and lived his life the best he could. It is for this reason that Beethoven will continue to live on in history.

Of course, his songs are still played today. From Moonlight Sonata, one of the most-played classical pieces in history, to the Ode to Joy, which symbolizes happiness and friendship for people across the world, no matter where you are from or what language you speak. Ode to Joy is spoken in a universal language: music.

Beethoven's songs have reached people across the globe. They have made people cry and smile and laugh and stand up and cheer. And, hopefully, they will continue to do so for centuries to come.